Presented to

By

Date

BREATH
PRAYERS

for Mothers

Simple Whispers That Keep You in God's Presence

HONOR 𝐇𝐁 BOOKS

Inspiration and Motivation for the Seasons of Life

An Imprint of Cook Communications Ministries • Colorado Springs, CO

08 07 06 05 04   10 9 8 7 6 5 4 3 2 1

Breath Prayers for Mothers—
Simple Whispers That Keep You in God's Presence
ISBN 1-56292-253-X

Copyright © 2004 Bordon Books
6532 East 71st St. Suite 105
Tulsa, OK 74133

Published by Honor Books,
An Imprint of Cook Communications Ministries
4050 Lee Vance View
Colorado Springs, CO 80918

Compiled and written by Edna G. Jordan
Designed by LJ Designs

Developed by Bordon Books

WHAT IS A BREATH PRAYER?

Even if you spent time in the morning with God, by the time you've finished item number ten on your list of things to do, the peace you previously felt may have evaporated; and perhaps He feels very far away. But He is as close as your breath; you can spend your entire day with Him—even on the run. Breath prayers are brief, heartfelt prayers that can help you enjoy God's company and surround your loved ones with prayer without retreating to the mountains and giving up your to-do list. The secret is a short prayer that you whisper to God as you go about your business, allowing your experiences to prompt you. As you see a friend, you can pray, "Father, bless her." As you stand in line, you can pray, "Father, bless her," for the cashier as someone argues with her. When you get to that three o'clock slump and wonder how you are going to get everything done, you can pray, "Father, bless me."

Instead of leaving God in the corner with your Bible, Breath prayers can help you live a life in which God walks with you throughout your day as you talk to Him about the things that cross your path. Your life will be transformed as you live continually in God's presence.

Best of all is it to preserve
everything in a pure, still heart,
and let there be for every
pulse a thanksgiving,
and for every breath a song.

Konrad von Gesner

Pray without ceasing.

1 Thessalonians 5:17 NKJV

How to Use
Breath Prayers for Mothers

After you have read **Breath Prayers for Mothers,** choose a prayer suitable for your use throughout the day. Repeat it so that you can say it to yourself in one breath, both in and out. Each breath is a prayer. In this way you will pray without ceasing and spend the entire day aware of God walking through each experience with you.

As you see people or think of them, as you experience situations or feelings, offer that prayer to God. "I exalt You, Lord," can become the refrain of your heart as you see drivers around you on the road, as you see various other people throughout your day. "I exalt You, Lord," can mean you celebrate with God the existence of others. It can mean you celebrate God's Lordship and loving care of them. It can also mean you praise God even though things are not going your way at the moment. The words will stay the same, but each breath you pray will be unique in the way you mean it to God. And you will maintain a constant connection with God.

[Pray] always with all prayer and supplication in the Spirit, being watchful to this end with all perseverance and supplication for all the saints.

EPHESIANS 6:18 NKJV

I LOOK TO YOU, LORD.

He will fulfill the desire of those who fear Him;
He will also hear their cry and will save them.

PSALM 145:19 NASB

It's another weekend and you're left at home all alone. Your husband has gone hunting with his buddies, and the kids are spending the night with friends. Your time is your own to do with as you please. That means you can kick back and relax, watch a movie, or maybe even read a book.

But looking around the big, empty house you realize you don't want to do any of those things. None of them can fill the emptiness—a void brought on because it seems as if you're always alone.

Lord, why can't my husband see that I need time alone with him? you wonder. *He's never here!*

Almighty God knew that man needed companionship when He created a woman and established the union of marriage (Genesis 2:18).

8

The intent was that the two would always be there for each other—to provide comfort to the other as well as be available to help out.

But in a fallen world, things don't always end up according to God's original design. Take heart. God is your sufficiency and you can count on Him to meet your needs, sometimes through your husband and sometimes in ways you would never have imagined. Trust in Him.

I can pray a breath prayer, *I look to You, Lord,* when—

- I am feeling lonely.

- I feel that I've failed.

- I don't understand how to do something.

- the children have repeatedly challenged my authority.

- I've been too busy.

- I feel as if I am not appreciated.

   I look to You, Lord.

JESUS, I COME TO
YOU FOR REST.

*Come to Me, all you who labor and are
heavy-laden and overburdened, and I will cause
you to rest. . . . Learn of Me . . . and you will
find rest (relief and ease and refreshment
and recreation and blessed quiet) for your souls.*

MATTHEW 11:28-29 AMP

It is often said that a man may work from
sunup to sundown, but a woman's work is never
done. Are you so busy that you seldom make
time to stop to take a breath each day?

The Bible says there is an appointed time for
everything—and that includes rest (Ecclesiastes 3:1
NASB). When the disciples were so busy they didn't
take time to eat, Jesus Christ took them away to
a quiet place so that they could rest (Mark 6:31).

After creation, even God rested on the seventh day.

Rest rejuvenates you and helps you think clearly. It also improves your disposition and aids in healing. Perhaps you have encouraged your toddler to have a quiet activity and a nap because you know the importance of "down time." Resting is healthy for those of all ages. Clear your mind and rest in God's presence.

I can pray a breath prayer, *Jesus, I come to You for rest,* when—

- I'm tired from the phone calls and visits since my baby was born.
- my baby wakes me up throughout the night.
- my child is sick.
- my baby is fretful because of teething.
- I'm tired from cleaning.
- I'm tired from running errands.
- I come home from work and have to care for my family.

Jesus, I come to You for rest.

LORD GOD, SHOW ME YOUR WAY.

"I am the Lord your God, who teaches you what is best for you, who directs you in the way you should go."

ISAIAH 48:17 NIV

We all have someone who has been a major influence in our lives. Usually, it is someone in our immediate family, possibly one of our parents. We all need someone to respect and trust— someone whose opinion we ask for and whose advice we follow.

However, no one could serve in that capacity in any greater way than Almighty God (Psalm 145:3) who has your family's path planned and worked out ahead of you. He already has the best answer and solution for every question, situation, and problem that you could encounter. Nothing is too big for Him. Neither is anything so small that He will not consider it. He is just waiting for you to ask Him (Psalm 91:15). He will direct your path and show you the way you should go.

I can pray a breath prayer, *Lord God, show me Your way,* when—

- my husband is offered a new job.
- we make financial decisions.
- we must move to a new location.
- we choose a school for our child.
- we need health care.
- we choose a church.

Lord God, show me Your way.

I RECEIVE YOUR PEACE, JESUS.

May the Lord of peace Himself grant you His peace . . . at all times and in all ways [under all circumstances and conditions, whatever comes].

2 THESSALONIANS 3:16 AMP

The world cannot give us true peace—only God can (John 14:27). However, the world is seeking peace wherever it can find it. Sadly, it is looking in the wrong places. John F. Kennedy said that peace lies in the hearts and minds of the people. God promised that when you present your requests to Him by prayer and with thanksgiving, His peace would guard your heart and your mind (Philippians 4:6-7 NIV).

God's desire is for you to have peace—within your own heart, with Him, and with others. He promised to bless you with peace (Psalm 29:11). When your mind seems full of troubled thoughts, focus your thoughts on the calm, quiet stillness of God's love for you.

I can pray a breath prayer, *I receive Your peace, Jesus,* when—

- I hear disturbing news.

- my husband travels out of town.

- there is conflict and confusion at my children's school.

- there are rumors of unemployment in the company.

- the weather is bad.

- others try to provoke my family.

- I know my children's hearts are troubled.

I receive Your peace, Jesus.

CREATOR, I PRAISE YOU FOR LIFE AND BREATH.

Let everything that has breath
and every breath of life praise the Lord!
Praise the Lord! (Hallelujah!)

PSALM 150:6 AMP

Excitement and expectation are with you everywhere you go now that you know you're going to have a baby. Every month, as the baby grows in your womb, you praise God for His creativity at work in both of your bodies.

You're in awe as you feel the baby move for the first time. As the child grows larger, the movement becomes stronger and more frequent as its temporary dwelling feels smaller and smaller. As both of you grow larger, you praise God that you are healthy and everything is going according to schedule.

You trust God, knowing He is well able to

handle any problem that might arise. Family and friends celebrate this new life with you and bless you with gifts. The nursery is beautifully decorated, waiting for its tiny tenant.

The staff and the birthing room are fully prepared for your arrival. You have prayed for a swift, uncomplicated delivery and recovery.

Now, the moment has arrived. You offer your baby's cry as praise unto God (Matthew 21:16 NASB).

I can pray a breath prayer, *Creator, I praise You for life and breath,* when—

- I go for my checkups.

- I feel the baby moving inside me.

- I see other mothers enjoying their children.

- complications arise.

- I prepare the nursery.

Creator, I praise You for life and breath.

DEVELOP YOUR PATIENCE IN ME, LORD!

*Let endurance and steadfastness
and patience have full play and do a
thorough work, so that you may be
[people] perfectly and fully developed.*

JAMES 1:4 AMP

Do you ever find yourself wishing you had another helping of patience? Perhaps the elderly lady in the grocery line in front of you who is counting her pennies is slowing you down. Maybe your child forgot to take their lunch to school and it threw your whole schedule off when you took it to them. Or what about the times you get stuck behind a school bus on your way to an appointment?

Patience is a product of love—preferring others and choosing kindness over frustration. God is always patient with you because He is love, and love is patient and kind. Patience is a fruit of the Spirit, and God will develop it in you if you allow Him to. But don't expect it to grow overnight. It takes time to develop it. However, it will grow as you practice it.

The next time you're ready to honk the horn at another driver or tell someone exactly how their delay has inconvenienced you, take a deep breath and practice patience.

I can pray a breath prayer, *Develop Your patience in me, Lord,* when—

- I am impatient with myself.

- I repeat the same mistakes.

- my child needs help with homework.

- my child has trouble learning something new.

- my child needs to be disciplined.

- I need to be patient with others.

Develop Your patience in me, Lord.

HOW PRECIOUS ARE YOUR THOUGHTS TO ME.

How precious also are Your thoughts to me, O God! How vast is the sum of them!
PSALM 139:17 NASB

God thinks about you every day, many times a day. It is good to remember this on a day when the laundry is taller than you are, and your children are fretful. God thinks of you. And He doesn't just think of you in passing; His thoughts dwell on you with great tenderness and compassion. After all, He designed you and made you. Why wouldn't He feel partial toward you?

God thinks of others too. As you go about your day, you can rejoice that the cashier with an attitude is on God's mind and heart, as is the neighbor next door in her grief. God's love for His creation is limitless.

The thoughts of God surround you and yours. One of His greatest desires is for your thoughts to be focused on Him in the same way. Pray this breath prayer to focus your attention on God, the Creator of the universe, and you will find that His love will grow more real to you as you go through your day.

I can pray a breath prayer, *How precious are Your thoughts to me,* when—

- I am lonely.
- I feel overwhelmed.
- I see a friend in need.
- my husband is preoccupied.
- my day is just beginning.

How precious are Your thoughts to me.

YOUR EYE IS ALWAYS UPON US, FATHER.

I will counsel you with My eye upon you.

PSALM 32:8 NASB

Three times this week, the person who is the teller at your bank has crossed your mind. The same thing happened yesterday when you thought about the woman who directs the choir in your church. Now, you can't stop thinking about that big business meeting your husband has to attend this afternoon.

Perhaps it's a gentle nudge from the Lord to say a prayer for them. While we may think all is well with the bank teller because she always has a smile for everyone, she may be going through some very difficult times. The rumors you heard about the choir director having a major illness may be true, though she never lets on that she is sick.

God prompts us to pray for others. In fact,

He encourages it in His Word (James 5:16).

Christ Jesus is always talking to the Father on your behalf (Hebrews 7:25), and God desires for you to pray for others. Just as He brings someone to your attention, you can be sure that He will bring your face or name to someone else's attention so that they can pray for you.

I can pray a breath prayer, *Your eye is always upon us, Father,* when—

- others cross my mind.

- I know someone has a need.

- I am tempted to pray for myself.

- a friend asks for prayer.

- someone has been mistreated.

- someone is going through a rough time.

Your eye is always upon us, Father.

TEACH ME TO KNOW YOUR VOICE.

My sheep recognize my voice;
I know them, and they follow me.

JOHN 10:27 NLT

God gave you the maternal instinct to know your child's cry from any other child's. Likewise, your child knows your voice from any other woman's. Before your children were born, they learned your voice. From the times that you sang lullabies to them while they were babies to yelling their name from the stands at school events, they know your voice.

When the prophet Samuel was a young boy, he helped Eli, the priest, in the temple. One night the Lord spoke to Samuel three times, but each time Samuel thought it was Eli's voice. After the third time, Eli realized it was the Lord trying to get Samuel's attention—teaching him to recognize His voice. Eli told Samuel to answer, "Yes, Lord, Your servant is listening." When he did, the Lord revealed to Samuel what was going to happen to Eli's family (1 Samuel 3:1-14 NLT).

As you pray with your children and read to them from the Bible, they learn to recognize God's voice and to respond to it, just as they did when they learned your voice.

I can pray a breath prayer, *Teach me to know Your voice,* when—

- You speak.

- my children pray.

- they read Your Word.

- the world seems loud and distracting.

- You give them instructions.

- You warn them.

- they are confused.

- others tell them what to do.

Teach me to know Your voice.

PUT YOUR SONG
IN MY HEART.

He has put a new song in my mouth.
PSALM 40:3 AMP

Whether it's played on an instrument or sung, whistled, or hummed, music touches the heart as nothing else can. It expresses your deepest feelings. You can probably place a particular song with each memorable event of your life—from the lullabies and nursery rhymes your mother sang when you were very young to your high school anthem and your first date. There were also the holidays, birthdays, graduations, weddings; and at times, the sad good-byes to someone very dear.

Wallace Stevens, an American poet, said that music is feeling, not sound. Your Heavenly Father takes such great delight in you that He rejoices over you with singing (Zephaniah 3:17 NIV). During those times with your child when words are not enough, rely on a song to express your love. It's an easy language to understand.

I can pray a breath prayer, *Put Your song in my heart,* when—

- someone has said something hurtful.

- I rock my baby to sleep.

- my child is afraid.

- my child is hurt.

- my child does not want me to leave.

- we travel.

- we play a game.

Put Your song in my heart.

GOD, HELP ME TO LOVE UNCONDITIONALLY.

The Lord your God has chosen you . . .
for Himself, a special treasure . . .
because the Lord loves you.

DEUTERONOMY 7:6,8 NKJV

It is comforting to know that you are loved and accepted because of who you are and not because of your portion in this life. In school, were you ever shunned because you did not wear the latest fashions? Or maybe you were favored because of who your parents were. You wanted to fit in because your classmates liked you, not because they wanted what you could give them or do for them.

God has entrusted you with the responsibility of letting your children know that they are loved and accepted by you and by Him. They are special regardless of the circumstances of their birth, their appearance, or anything else. Let them know that their performance—good or bad—does not determine your love and acceptance of them.

God's love and acceptance of you is based on His loving grace. He looks past the flaws, the good or the bad, and accepts you through Christ Jesus (Ephesians 1:6).

I can pray a breath prayer, *God, help me to love unconditionally,* when—

- I am told that my children have special needs.

- they grow and develop slower than other children.

- they have behavioral problems.

- they disappoint me.

- others reject them.

- others say their best is not good enough.

God, help me to love unconditionally.

ORDER MY LIFE, LORD.

Do everything properly and in order.
1 CORINTHIANS 14:40 CEV

It is easy to become involved with so much busyness from day to day that your life falls out of proper order. Your emotions are overwhelming, threatening to drag you under. Or perhaps things are changing so rapidly around you that you feel you're off balance.

God wants to help balance you and offer His steady hand to help you put things in proper order. Much like a parent teaching their child to walk, He stands firm and solid, Someone you can hold to steady yourself.

You can rest assured that God is available to help you wisely handle your daily life—keeping

people, places, and things in proper order
(Proverbs 16:20 KJV). He stands ready to direct
you and show you what things are most important.
Let Him help you set your "to do" list.

I can pray a breath prayer, *Order my life, Lord,*
when—

- I am not spending enough time with my
  child.

- I experience a lot of pressure on my job.

- I spend too much time away from home.

- something unexpected happens that I
  don't feel prepared for.

- I have many errands to run.

- I do not know how to relax.

- my doctor warns me to take it easy.

Order my life, Lord.

LORD, PROTECT MY LOVED ONES.

I will give safety to your children.
ISAIAH 49:25 AMP

Most mothers, human and animal, will defend their young, even to the point of sacrificing their own lives. You instinctively know when your children are threatened, and you will do whatever is necessary to protect them.

When you are expecting your baby, you obey your doctor for your baby's sake more than your own. You feel confident that they are healthy and safe because you are doing what is necessary to ensure it. You are the one who is directly responsible for their life.

Your child is just as precious to God. As you pray for your child, you express your faith in

God to keep that child safe.

When you are not always around to care for him, warn him, and protect him, rest assured that Almighty God is always there—from babyhood to adulthood. The Lord sees clearly what your child is doing (Proverbs 5:21 NLT). He watches over your child as his protector, deliverer (Psalm 50:15), and Savior.

I can pray a breath prayer, *Lord, protect my loved ones,* when—

- they are still in the womb.

- they are at home.

- they are at day care and school.

- they are with friends.

- they travel without me.

- they grow up and become adults.

Lord, protect my loved ones.

I WILL BE CONTENT IN YOU, FATHER.

Don't grumble as some of them did.

1 CORINTHIANS 10:10 NLT

You wanted an SUV, but your husband bought a truck. The house you live in has three bedrooms, but you could really use five. Dinner is always hamburger, chicken, or fish. "Can't we have steak just once in a while?" you ask.

It's OK to be disappointed at times. What is important, though, is how you handle that disappointment.

When God brought the Israelites out of bondage, He promised them a bountiful, rich land. He also desired that they rest and enjoy the abundance of His love and provision. But they soon grew tired of eating the same old food and started to complain.

On the other hand, Paul looked at what was

going on in his life and decided to be content (Philippians 4:11), knowing that God would provide whatever he needed, whenever he needed it.

Your Heavenly Father is filled with goodness. When you recognize His goodness in each area of your life, you can find many reasons to be content with where you are on the path to where He's taking you.

I can pray a breath prayer, *I will be content in You, Father,* when—

- I am disappointed.

- situations become uncomfortable.

- my husband disagrees concerning a purchase.

- I can't get things I want.

- I am tired.

- someone mistreats me.

- my prayers are not answered quickly.

I will be content in You, Father.

THANK YOU FOR YOUR MANY GIFTS.

*Children are a gift from the Lord;
they are a reward from him.*

PSALM 127:3 NLT

How do you treat a gift? If it is something you really appreciate and desire, you handle it with great care. Perhaps you display it proudly. Or maybe you keep it for your eyes only. It is close to your heart—not because of its monetary value, but because it cost the giver something valuable. You see beauty in its flaws—not necessarily in its perfection. It is special because of who gave it to you.

Your child is a gift from God. Every living soul belongs to Him (Ezekiel 18:4 NIV), and He has specifically entrusted you with the care and training of this child. This is not easy to believe when it has been some time since you saw the living-room carpet free of toys. But, your Heavenly Father desires that your child will enhance your life with joy and pleasure—just like any other precious gift. Your child was fashioned by God's hand specifically for you.

I can pray a breath prayer, *Thank You for Your many gifts,* when—

- I receive news of an unplanned pregnancy.

- I do not know how I will be able to provide for the baby.

- others criticize me for having another child.

- my child's energy level surpasses mine.

- my children disobey and anger me.

- my children make me proud.

Thank You for Your many gifts.

ALL AUTHORITY COMES FROM YOU, LORD.

*Give respect and honor
to all to whom it is due.*

ROMANS 13:7 NLT

God established authority. Christ Jesus gave a wonderful example of honoring authority when He humbled himself to God's will and died for us.

God has given instructions for children to honor and obey their parents first of all (Ephesians 6:2). As your child grows, he will learn to honor others with authority in your family, neighborhood, at school, and at church. As you teach him, pray that he will understand that God established rules and laws, lawmakers, and law enforcers for our peace and welfare

(Romans 13:1; 1 Peter 2:13-14).

Lead by example. As you obey the laws of the land and those God has placed in authority in your life, your child will follow your example.

I can pray a breath prayer, *All authority comes from You, Lord,* when—

- my children are with family, friends, and neighbors.

- those in authority seem to be wrong.

- a decision of one in authority impacts my child in a negative way.

- others ridicule those in authority.

- my child needs correction.

All authority comes from You, Lord.

FATHER, MAY I SEEK YOUR WISDOM.

Learn to be wise, and develop good judgment. . . . Getting wisdom is the most important thing you can do!

PROVERBS 4:5,7 NLT

"If only I had known back then what I know now!" We cannot travel back in time, but we can be thankful that we have learned from our past mistakes. As a loving mother, you do not want your children to make the same mistakes that you made. That is why you constantly teach them to choose what God says is right.

While babies, they totally depend on your judgment. As they grow, you gradually allow them enough freedom to make their own choices. You help them consider beforehand what the results of their decision might be and help them prepare to handle the outcome.

You pray for them to grow strong and increase in wisdom, and that God's grace will be upon them (Luke 2:40 NASB). Then you will be glad and your heart will rejoice as they mature into a responsible adult (Proverbs 23:25 NIV).

I can pray a breath prayer, *Father, may I seek Your wisdom,* when—

- my children have to make hard decisions and solve difficult problems.

- they learn to do chores at home.

- they interact with others at school.

- they form lasting friendships.

- they join extracurricular activities.

- they choose a career or college.

- I am unsure what to do.

    Father, may I seek Your wisdom.

WISDOM AND KNOWLEDGE ARE FOUND IN YOU, GOD.

*God gave these four young men
an unusual aptitude for learning the
literature and science of the time.*

DANIEL 1:17 NLT

Daniel, Shadrach, Meshach, and Abednego were young Israelites who were taken captive by Nebuchadnezzar, a Babylonian king who worshipped idols. They worshipped God, but the king chose them to be trained to serve in his royal court. They were the best—strong, healthy, good-looking, well versed in every branch of learning, gifted with knowledge and good sense, and with the poise to serve in his palace (Daniel 1:4 NLT).

They probably resented their situation, but they trusted God and were willing to learn. God graced them with more knowledge, intelligence,

42

and skill than their peers. The king was so impressed with them that he put them on his staff of advisors, and their counsel was ten times wiser than all of his magicians and enchanters.

In a way, it reminds you of the rewards of higher education. God wants your child's mind to be strong, healthy, and sound. You want your children to take advantage of every opportunity that God gives them to develop intellectually and scholastically. Encourage your children to be willing and obedient to learn more so that they will experience God's best.

I can pray a breath prayer, *Wisdom and knowledge are found in You, God,* when—

- my children are at home, school, and church.

- they are introduced to something new.

- they feel bored.

- they feel like a failure.

- a new environment surrounds them.

Wisdom and knowledge are found in You, God.

LIGHT MY PATH, GOD.

By Your words I can see where I'm going;
they throw a beam of light on my dark path.

PSALM 119:105 MSG

"Mommy, it's dark in here! I can't see!"
Has the power in your home ever gone out during
a storm and you heard your child cry those
words from the darkness of their bedroom?
While you stumbled in the dark to get to them,
did you stub your toe or trip over something?
What a terrifying feeling it is to have to grope
around in the dark, not knowing what is in front
of you, or even if you're headed in the right
direction! Living life without the light of God's
Word is much like trying to find your way in
the dark.

You don't have to sit in the dark wondering about your life and God's direction for your family. Thank and praise God because He has set a path before you and it shines brighter with each step (Proverbs 4:18 NIV) as you follow God, because His Word is the lamp to your feet and the light to your path (Psalm 119:105).

I can pray a breath prayer, *Light my path, God,* when—

- I don't know which direction to go.

- I falter.

- I am unsure if I made the right decision.

- I feel my actions were hurtful or painful to others.

- I am tempted to fear.

- my family doesn't understand.

Light my path, God.

LORD, GIVE ME A HEART
FOR RIGHTEOUSNESS.

Even a child is known by his actions,
by whether his conduct is pure and right.

PROVERBS 20:11 NIV

"Be sure and be on your best behavior!"
"Make Mommy proud!"

We teach our children good manners at
home so that in public, or when we are not
around, they will behave well.

The Bible says that a good reputation is
worth much more than silver and gold (Proverbs
22:1 CEV). When you hear the name of Jesus,
you immediately think of the wonderful things
He did. Everything He said and did represented
God's love for the world.

Likewise, your children represent you—your

behavior, values, and habits that you have taught them, intentionally or not. It is said that first impressions are lasting impressions. Teaching your child good behavior and enforcing it will leave others with a good impression of both your child and you. Most of all, God is pleased; and as your child grows up, his good name will precede him.

I can pray a breath prayer, *Lord, give me a heart for righteousness,* when—

- others are watching.

- no one is watching but You.

- my child is in someone else's care.

- my child faces peer pressure.

- my child is disciplined.

- my child leads others.

- others ask for their help.

Lord, give me a heart for righteousness.

FATHER, LEAD ME TO DEPEND ON YOU.

Where will I find help? It will come from the Lord, who created the heavens and the earth.

PSALM 121:1-2 CEV

As infants, children are very dependent on you. They need your help for everything—to feed, bathe, clothe, carry, protect, provide for, and comfort them. As they grow they struggle to find their independence. They become less dependent on you, but you assure them that you are there in case they need your help.

However, there will be times in life when you won't be able to be there for your child, but God will always be there. God desires for all of us to depend on Him. Slowly you transfer your child's dependence on you to God instead. As your children grow, encourage them to understand that their Heavenly Father is always there to help, no matter what they need (Psalm 46:1; Hebrews 4:16).

I can pray a breath prayer, *Father, lead me to depend on You.* when—

- my children need someone to talk to.

- they feel hopeless

- they are struggling under pressure

- they are about to say or do something wrong

- no one is there to help them.

- no one believes they are telling the truth.

    Father, lead me to depend on You.

BE LORD OF MY RELATIONSHIPS, FATHER.

Lord . . . I promise to obey your words!
Anyone who fears you is my friend—
anyone who obeys your commandments.

PSALM 119:57,63 NLT

There are many stories of friendship in the Bible. Abraham is called a friend of God (James 2:23). Jonathan, the son of Saul, and David were covenant brothers in spite of Saul's attempts to kill David. God desires for you and your children to have good friends who share your love for Him.

Your child will begin to meet people and develop friendships as a toddler. As your children grow, you teach them the difference between right and wrong relationships. At first, you choose their playmates and friends. But gradually, with your guidance, you allow them to choose their own friends. And you will want to be careful for yourself as well.

First Corinthians 15:33 NLT says that bad company corrupts good character, but the right friends will encourage you or your child to do what is right (Proverbs 27:17 AMP).

I can pray a breath prayer, *Be Lord of my relationships, Father,* when—

- I introduce my children to someone new.

- others try to influence them with peer pressure.

- they begin dating.

- they need support and encouragement from others.

- I meet new people.

- I'm tempted to discard friends.

  Be Lord of my relationships, Father.

FATHER, MAKE ME DILIGENT TO LEARN AND TEACH.

You must commit yourselves wholeheartedly to these commands I am giving you today. Repeat them again and again to your children. Talk about them when you are at home and when you are away on a journey, when you are lying down and when you are getting up again.

DEUTERONOMY 6:6-7 NLT

When you were learning something new you were more than likely told, "Practice makes perfect!" If you grew tired or became frustrated when you messed up, most likely you were encouraged to try again. Eventually, you got the hang of it and achieved your goal.

Life's lessons are usually learned through experience. You would prefer that your children not learn lessons in the proverbial "school of hard knocks," because most consequences learned from those lessons are unpleasant. Should that happen, use God's Word to help them understand why things turned out the way they did.

Sometimes you will wipe away their tears. Others times you will apply "tough love." God will help you to lovingly and tirelessly persevere even when your children repeat errors. His Word promises that when you teach your children to choose the right path, they will remain on it when they are older (Proverbs 22:6 NLT).

I can pray a breath prayer, *Father, make me diligent to learn and teach,* when—

- my children do not want to listen.
- I am unsure of what my children need to know.
- they want to be like their friends.
- they are confused.
- their feelings are hurt.
- they want to get even.
- they make the same mistakes again and again.

Father, make me diligent to learn and teach.

LORD, I RELY ON YOU TO KEEP ME SAFE.

You will be secure, because there is hope; you will look about you and take your rest in safety.

JOB 11:18 NIV

When America's security was breached on September 11, 2001, we realized that our nation was not invincible and that our security measures were not infallible. Some felt it best to take responsibility for their own safety. But terrorism has more than one face, and there are many avenues of self-defense. So, where do you begin? How do you prepare for your family's protection so that they feel secure?

Psalm 91:2,4, and 14 assure you that your Heavenly Father is your refuge and fortress. He will rescue, protect, and shield you. His faithful promises are your armor. He watches over you and He hears your prayers (1 Peter 3:12 NLT), so follow His instructions when He shows you what to do and put your family trust in Him (Psalm 118:8 NLT). You can rest knowing He has made a way for you.

I can pray a breath prayer, *Lord, I rely on You to keep me safe,* when—

- my husband is out of town.

- my husband is laid off from his job.

- my authority is challenged.

- my faith is tested.

- my family is threatened.

- others take care of our children.

- I hear bad news reports.

Lord, I rely on You to keep me safe.

MAY MY WORDS REFLECT YOUR TRUTH.

Speak the truth to each other.

ZECHARIAH 8:16 NIV

"The check is in the mail." "That's not what I said." "No one will know I took it, anyway." "I'll pay you back." "It's not my fault she gave me too much change."

It's so easy to tell a lie or justify wrongdoing when you find yourself in a tight spot. That's a temptation everyone faces sooner or later.

But God's Word, the same Word you have inside you, is truth. If it is impossible for Him to lie, it should be the same with you.

Just as you put confidence in Him and His truthfulness, He expects you to do the same. He is looking to you to be an example before others—beginning with your spouse and children.

Pray a breath prayer to Him to help you guard your words and always be truthful, no matter how difficult the situation may be. You please Him when you are willing to be responsible for your actions and live honest lives.

Always speak the truth.

I can pray a breath prayer, *May my words reflect Your truth,* when—

- my husband or child asks me a question.

- I handle my finances.

- I know it might get me in trouble.

- I am asked to lie.

- I must explain my actions.

- I prepare my taxes.

- I am tempted to justify my actions.

May my words reflect Your truth.

GIVE ME A HEART
OF OBEDIENCE, GOD.

Children, obey your parents because you belong
to the Lord, for this is the right thing to do.

EPHESIANS 6:1 NLT

When someone disobeys God, it means that
he does not honor Him or trust that His Word is
true. That grieves the Holy Spirit and separates
the person from God. Adam and Eve's disobedience separated them from God and made every
curse imaginable fall on humanity.

Christ Jesus, on the other hand, was obedient—first to Joseph and Mary, who were His
earthly parents, and also to Almighty God, His
Heavenly Father. His obedience made salvation
available for mankind.

Obedience is a command from God. When
your child obeys you, it shows respect for your
leadership and also his trust that what you say

and do is right. Therefore, he is willing to do whatever you tell him. His obedience also ensures your close relationship and makes life pleasant for both of you.

As your child loves and obeys you, he also learns to love and obey God. And God's promise of a long, good life will follow him (Ephesians 6:3).

I can pray a breath prayer, *Give me a heart of obedience, God,* when—

- what I ask my children seems difficult.

- they are tempted to follow the crowd.

- they are angry or afraid.

- the right thing to do isn't crystal clear.

- other children are allowed to do something that goes against our rules.

Give me a heart of obedience, God.

IN YOUR PRESENCE THERE IS LOVE, FATHER.

A capable, intelligent, and virtuous woman . . . looks well to how things go in her household.

PROVERBS 31:10,27 AMP

Home. The word should bring good thoughts to your mind. If you are tired from a hectic week of work, you think of rest. If you travel and eat out a lot, you think of a home-cooked meal. If you face obnoxious people all week, you think of love. And if you want a temporary escape from bad news, you think of the peace that awaits you at home.

A good home provides the suitable atmosphere for spiritual, mental, emotional, physical, and domestic well-being. A house can be large, immaculately clean, filled with beautiful, expensive furnishings, and still lack qualities that make it a good home.

It is said that home is where the heart is. Invite your Heavenly Father to be the center—the heart—of your home. And then ask Him for the knowledge, skill, and creativity to make your home a happy place for your family.

I can pray a breath prayer, *In Your presence there is love, Father,* when—

- we need down time to relax.

- we have guests.

- I feel as if I can't keep up with everything I need to do.

- there is tension in our home.

- we do not have everything that we need.

- the children are facing pressures outside our home.

In Your presence there is love, Father.

IN YOUR ORDER, THERE IS JOY.

Seek (aim at and strive after) first of all His kingdom and His righteousness (His way of doing and being right), and then all these things taken together will be given you besides.

MATTHEW 6:33 AMP

Samuel Smiles, a Scottish writer, said, "A place for everything, and everything in its place." It is important that you put things in proper order in your life and teach your child to do the same.

When your child is young, what is important to him is whatever makes him feel good and makes him happy. God trusts you to teach your child to place everyone and everything in life where they should be according to His Word. Most important, your children will learn how precious life is—how God values our lives so much that He sent Christ Jesus to die for us—and they will love and revere Jesus as Lord.

Your children will be thankful for the loving family and friends who enrich their lives. They will understand that God is pleased when they prosper (Psalm 35:27) and that God is the One who gives them the good things in life (James 1:17). However, they will realize that these things can be enjoyed most when put in their rightful place.

I can pray a breath prayer, *In Your order, there is joy,* when—

- household chores are required.

- they have schoolwork to complete.

- they have a job.

- they plan for the future.

- I want to rethink my priorities.

In Your order, there is joy.

YOU ARE MY HOPE, LORD.

Why are you downcast, O my soul?
Why so disturbed within me?
Put your hope in God, for I will yet
praise him, my Savior.

PSALM 42:5 NIV

Hopelessness. You can see it in the faces of so many people. Maybe you see it in your own face today as you look in the mirror. Perhaps you are facing a crisis and all the facts say that it's all over, so you might as well give up. Or are you facing a situation that has been going on for so long that you have become weary and no longer see any reason to be hopeful? Does there appear to be no way out? Have you lost all hope?

Well, if that describes you, there's good news. There is always hope with God. Even when the circumstances say otherwise, you can hope against hope, because God can and does work miracles. Your situation may be beyond the help of man, but God is your hope and He is working on your behalf.

I can pray a breath prayer, *You are my hope, Lord,* when—

- I see no way out.

- no person can do anything to help.

- my emotions are spiraling downward.

- I can't do anything to change my situation.

- I need a miracle.

- all appears to be lost.

You are my hope, Lord.

GIVE ME A
DILIGENT HEART.

*Lazy people want much but get little, but those
who work hard will prosper and be satisfied.*

PROVERBS 13:4 NLT

God desires your diligence—painstaking,
constant, and persevering effort, and hard work.
Moses instructed the Israelites to diligently obey
God's commands (Deuteronomy 6:17). The
apostle Paul warned Christians about being lazy
and idle. He encouraged them to work so that
they would not be a burden to others (2 Thessalonians 3:6-8 NLT).

When you make a commitment, it is important to follow through. Your word bears your
reputation. You are known by the value of your
word. Are you on time? Do you keep appoint-
ments? Can others always count on you?

Diligence takes effort. Your Heavenly Father

desires to see you succeed. Ask Him to help you do your work with a fresh excitement as if you were working directly for Him. He can help you complete every task with excellence. Then listen to hear Him prompt your heart when time gets away from you or you've forgotten something. He's ready to help you.

I can pray a breath prayer, *Give me a diligent heart*, when—

- I am tempted to put off my housework.

- I have made a commitment and am tempted not to keep it.

- my children are watching and I am not aware of it.

- I make promises to others.

- I see an opportunity to help someone else succeed.

Give me a diligent heart.

I ENTRUST ALL TO YOU, FATHER.

"I prayed for this child, and the Lord has
granted me what I asked of him.
So now I give him to the Lord. For his whole
life he will be given over to the Lord."

1 SAMUEL 1:27-28 NIV

Are you hesitant to leave your child in someone else's care? Maybe you feel that someone
else might not understand the meaning of each
whine, cry, frown, pout, and smile like you do,
and that they might not respond in the right
way. But you know that you cannot be with
your child all the time, and sooner or later you
are going to have to let go.

Remember that when you do let go, your
Heavenly Father does not. He is right there when
you can't be there. He loves your child more
than you can imagine. He created them, watched
over them, and took care of them before they

were born; and He will do it now. He will hear and answer their cry when you cannot (Psalm 145:19).

Give every concern about your child's welfare to God (1 Peter 5:7). Do not be anxious or worried (Philippians 4:6). Instead, pray about everyone and everything that will touch their life. Thank God for His provision and protection over your child and leave them in His capable hands.

I can pray a breath prayer, *I entrust all to You, Father,* when—

- I have to trust someone else with the care of my children.
- they are with family and friends.
- they travel.
- they are influenced by teachers, coaches, and other adults.
- I have a job interview.
- I have to focus my attention on work or other activities.

I entrust all to You, Father.

SUCCESS IS FROM YOU, LORD.

*He [the Lord] will make you successful
in everything you do.*

DEUTERONOMY 28:12 CEV

No one wants to be a failure or a loser.
We have a deeply rooted drive to conquer and to
excel. Unfortunately, there are times we all try
to succeed within our own natural power and
ability. You were never created to succeed
without God's help. It is not that He is holding
you back, but rather that He is your Creator
who gave you life; apart from Him you can do
nothing (John 15:5).

Let your child know that God wants him to
succeed (Deuteronomy 28:13) and that He is
right there to help him. Encourage him to give his

best effort, and trust God to take it from there.

I can pray a breath prayer, *Success is from You, Lord*, when—

- things don't come easily to my children.

- they study and prepare for tests.

- given the opportunity to help others.

- achievement seems too hard and they are tempted to give up.

- I wonder about my parenting.

- the finish line seems far off.

Success is from You, Lord.

FATHER GOD, YOU
PLAY NO FAVORITES.

*"I now realize how true it is
that God does not show favoritism
but accepts men from every nation who
fear him and do what is right."*

ACTS 10:34-35 NIV

Aren't you glad that God loves you best?
But then He also loves everyone else best too.
And that is why we all feel so secure in His love.
He doesn't play favorites unless it is to make us
all His favorites.

Your loved ones will all feel secure in your
love if, like God, you show no partiality. And
your friends will rely on you when they know
that your love is firm and fair, even when things
get hot.

But this kind of love comes only from God. You'll want to spend time with Him—lots of time—before you'll find yourself loving like Him with fairness. You can do this with a breath prayer.

I can pray a breath prayer, *Father God, You play no favorites*, when—

- someone poor or different shows up in my neighborhood.

- I give gifts to my children.

- my children seek my approval.

- I'm tempted to favor people at church who are like me.

- I discipline my children.

- my personality clashes with one child and not the other.

Father God, You play no favorites.

WE BELONG
TO YOU, FATHER.

I am praying for them . . .
for those You have given Me,
for they belong to You.

JOHN 17:9 AMP

Have you ever seen the look of pride on a child's face when his father comes out on top in front of his friends? The look on his face says, "That's my Dad!" and he wants the whole world to know it. To a child, his parent is the best and no other parent comes close.

Your children love you and feel that way about you. They are glad that you are their mother and are proud to be your children. As you read the Bible to them and teach them about their Heavenly Father, they will learn that they

are also God's child (Romans 8:16). And they
will be happy and feel honored that they belong
to God. You can be glad that you belong to Him
too.

I can pray a breath prayer, *We belong to You,
Father,* when—

- I am proud of something I or my children
  have done.

- others make fun of me or my children.

- my husband and I face a difficult decision.

- someone has hurt our family.

- my children are the hit of the party.

- my husband and I make a decision to cut
  down on television and video games as a
  family.

We belong to You, Father.

LORD, REMIND ME OF YOUR LOVE.

*You have loved them [even]
as You have loved Me.*

JOHN 17:23 AMP

Rejection is very painful and can cause deep emotional wounds. No one wants to feel that they are not good enough or that they have to earn acceptance and love. Regretfully, that happens.

But God is not like that. Before He created the world, He loved you and chose you to be part of His family (Ephesians 1:4-5 NLT). His love and acceptance are not based on anything you have done (Romans 11:6 AMP).

Just as you assure your children that you love them unconditionally—just because of who they are and not for what they have done—also teach them that Almighty God loves them and accepts them in Christ Jesus. They do not have to earn His love; God has the same love for them that He has for Christ Jesus. God has the same love for you too.

I can pray a breath prayer, *Lord, remind me of Your love,* when—

- relationships with others seem difficult.

- my children get hurt by a friend.

- I want desperately to be understood.

- I know my actions disappointed You.

- I am in a new environment and friendly faces seem hard to find.

- someone reaches out in friendship.

Lord, remind me of Your love.

LORD, MAY I FALL IN LOVE WITH YOU.

Love God, your God, with your whole heart: love him with all that's in you, love him with all you've got!

DEUTERONOMY 6:5 MSG

It is regrettable that the word "love"—the very word that God uses to describe himself—is so misused and misunderstood. The meaning of the word has become shallow in our language today. Love is used to express feelings for just about everything including food, pets, clothes, cars, sports, and entertainment. "I love those jeans you're wearing." "I love vacationing in the country." "I love chocolate chip cookies." And on and on it goes.

Your child will pursue interests and develop relationships their entire life, and some will be more special to them than others. As your child discovers how much God loves them, they will realize how special God's love is for them and that nothing can compare with it. God will become more dear to them and they will become devoted to God. God will be their first love.

I can pray a breath prayer, *Lord, may I fall in love with You,* when—

- my children develop relationships with others.

- they are with others who do not love You.

- their emotions get the best of them.

- I or my children do not feel close to You.

- I am tempted to doubt Your love.

- we experience Your compassion for others.

- my heart feels hard and cold toward You and others.

Lord, may I fall in love with You.

I ENDURE IN YOUR STRENGTH, LORD.

I press on toward the goal to win the prize for which God has called me.

PHILIPPIANS 3:14 NIV

"I can't do it!" You smile and take your child's hand and say, "Yes, you can. Let's try it again." Thank God that He is so patient and kind that He also holds our hands as we keep trying until we get things right.

God told Joshua to lead the Israelites and destroy the city of Jericho (Joshua 6:1-21). He instructed them to march around the city for seven days and then He told them that the walls would collapse so they could charge into the city. The Israelites obeyed and the walls fell, just as God said they would. Then they captured Jericho, but it happened only because they kept at it day after day like God told them to do.

There are days when your tasks are fulfilled with ease. But more often than not you face challenges every day that may not seem worth the effort. Your efforts will not go unnoticed, however. Your Heavenly Father sees your heart and knows how hard some things can be. But when you push through by refusing to give up, the reward is sweet.

I can pray a breath prayer, *I endure in Your strength, Lord,* when—

- I feel like disciplining my child is a losing battle.

- I'm tired of being the "bad" parent, always saying "no."

- it feels as if I can't win.

- others tell me to give up.

- I feel that no one is supporting me.

- I feel like I can't hear You, God.

I endure in Your strength, Lord.

SHOW ME YOUR
GOODNESS, LORD.

*Open your mouth and taste, open your
eyes and see—how good God is.*

PSALM 34:8 MSG

Life is full of ups and downs, which can
weigh heavily on your emotions. Life does have
its share of hardships, but you don't have to let
them get you down. As you gather a glimpse of
God's goodness, you gain a fresh perspective that
can counter discouragement when things don't
go as you planned, or you can keep a positive
point of view when trouble comes knocking.

God does not want you to allow the troubled
times to block your view of what great blessings
you have in Him. Even in tough times, He wants
you to remember that He is always there for you
and He has promised to cause all things to work

together for good because you love Him (Romans 8:28).

He has also promised that you would be satisfied with His goodness (Jeremiah 31:14). So, regardless of how things seem—no matter how rough times might get—God will keep His word. Expect Him to show you His goodness, and watch for it to unfold before you.

I can pray a breath prayer, *Show me Your goodness, Lord,* when—

- I can't take any more bad news.

- others have treated me with cruelty.

- I don't know what to do next.

- I feel as if things can't get any worse.

- I feel distraught.

- I can't find the right words when I pray.

Show me Your goodness, Lord.

MAY MY LIFE REFLECT YOUR GLORY, JESUS.

*Be an example to all believers in what
you teach, in the way you live.*

1 TIMOTHY 4:12 NLT

A good leader does their best to be sure that
what they say and what they do go hand in
hand. It is easier to follow someone who lives
what they say they believe. You trust the leader
who is a living example of what they teach.

As a parent, you gain your child's confidence
when your actions follow your words. Your
consistency helps them to be truthful and develop
stability without confusion or frustration.
Whether you praise them or discipline them,
they will trust you because they witness no compromise or double standards in your life.

Christ Jesus did exactly what God told Him

to do. He followed the same truth that He taught His disciples. He truly practiced what He preached.

Your desire to lead by a good example is honorable. As you follow Christ, you become His example and can be confident when others follow you as you follow Christ.

I can pray a breath prayer, *May my life reflect Your glory, Jesus*, when—

- I need to ask for forgiveness from You and others.

- I am tempted to let my emotions control me.

- I am given a compliment.

- someone points out my mistakes.

- someone treats me wrong.

- someone needs my help.

- I win or lose a game.

May my life reflect Your glory, Jesus.

MAY I DISCIPLINE IN LOVE, FATHER.

Those whom the LORD loves He disciplines.

HEBREWS 12:6 NASB

Perhaps you have repeatedly watched your child deliberately disobey and then issued a threat of punishment knowing full well you would not carry it out. Most of us have done it.

Why do we shrink and shrivel when it comes to punishing our children? We aren't afraid of our child, but perhaps we try to protect the relationship that exists between us.

Discipline is a big part of love when it comes to raising children. God, our Heavenly Father, loves us. Just as you expect your own child to follow your expectations, God expects us to obey His instructions. When we do something wrong, we suffer the consequences of that wrongdoing. That's where His correction and forgiveness benefit us.

God can help you help your child understand that disobedience cannot go unpunished. Purpose to take a stand and hand out discipline when it is needed. Your child and you will both benefit from your commitment.

I can pray a breath prayer, *May I discipline in love, Father,* when—

- my child disobeys me.
- it comes to disciplining my child.
- my child begs me to give in to their request.
- what my children want to do could be dangerous.
- they are held accountable for their actions at school.
- I need to support other authorities in their lives.
- they have deliberately deceived me.

May I discipline in love, Father.

LET YOUR GENTLENESS LEAD ME.

A gentle answer turns away wrath,
but a harsh word stirs up anger.

PROVERBS 15:1 NASB

"But everybody's doing it!"

How many times have you heard that from your child?

He wants to go away for the weekend with some friends from school. In judgmental fashion, you are quick to suggest that such trips only lead to trouble.

At 15, she feels she is old enough to start dating. Your response is an emphatic "No." He's ready to hit the road, but in his own car. Instead of encouraging him to wait a couple of years until he's older, you compare him to other teens his age and say he's not mature enough to have his driver's license.

Giving quick responses to requests that hold so much importance to your child fails to communicate your love and affection in a positive way. Children always want to hear "Yes" when they take requests to their parents. But if the answer has to be "No," sprinkle it with love, a listening ear, and show signs that you have your child's interest at heart. They are more likely to accept your "No" with little question.

I can pray a breath prayer, *Let Your gentleness lead me,* when—

- I know my "no" is in my child's best interest.

- I don't feel comfortable about a matter.

- my child is insistent.

- other parents are saying yes.

- I feel an urge to compromise.

- I know my child is over-committed already.

Let Your gentleness lead me.

GOD, GIVE ME A HEART
OF ENCOURAGEMENT.

*I thought it necessary to
exhort the brethren.*

2 CORINTHIANS 9:5 KJV

Most children can be easily persuaded,
particularly when they are trying to "fit in." Few
children have true confidence in themselves or
their own abilities.

That's why it is important that you, as a
mother and a parent, encourage your children.

When God called Moses to deliver the message of deliverance to Pharaoh, Moses responded
that he was inadequate and that he was not an
eloquent speaker (Exodus 4:10). But God saw
something in Moses that His servant obviously
did not see in himself.

In response, God promised to be with
Moses. He also said that He would teach Moses.

90

Not only are your children a gift to you from God, but they come complete with gifts and talents that they can use to be a blessing to others. Your words of love and encouragement will develop confidence in God's ability to fulfill His purpose for them.

I can pray a breath prayer, *God, give me a heart of encouragement*, when—

- my child has little or no self-confidence.

- no one else is supportive.

- others make fun of them.

- the task seems to be more than they can handle.

- it would be easier to do the job myself.

- my child fears failure.

God, give me a heart of encouragement.

HELP ME LET GO, LORD.

Train a child in the way he should go.

PROVERBS 22:6 NIV

Driving away from the college campus the first time, you fight to hold back the tears that have threatened to appear all day. Your thoughts do not dwell as much on your child's having finally left home, so much as on what life was like when you had them at home with you.

Your child was safe, because you did your best to keep them from harm. You always made sure they had meals at home and lunches at school. During those young, tender years you did just what God intended. You trained your child and taught them the meaning of being responsible.

Now comes the more difficult part. It's time to let go. You've been doing it gradually all along. But now it's time to turn loose even more, step back, and see what all those years of teaching and training will produce.

I can pray a breath prayer, *Help me let go, Lord,* when—

- it's time for my child to step out on his own.

- my child wants to do things for herself.

- my child feels smothered by my eagerness to help.

- I still feel responsible for my child.

- I know it's time to let my child go.

- I need to let my worries go and trust You.

Help me let go, Lord.

LET ME SEE WITH YOUR EYES.

So God created man in his own image.

GENESIS 1:27 KJV

No child of mine would ever do something so foolish. How many times has that thought crossed your mind? We can be so surprised by some of the things our children do.

There is a lot of truth to the old saying, "Kids will be kids." Recalling his own childhood, the apostle Paul referred to many of his actions as "childish" (1 Corinthians 13:11). But when he grew up, Paul put aside those childish things and began to act more responsibly.

Though He may be disappointed in us, God is never surprised when we draw the wrong conclusion, make incorrect decisions, or act foolishly. Instead, He looks at us through His Son, Jesus, with eyes of forgiveness. That way,

He sees potential—who we can become instead of what we are now.

We can have a powerful impact on our own children by seeing them as God sees them. When we trade criticism for a heart of compassion and stand ready to forgive, we can send a message of expectation that will cause our children to fly higher in their own hearts.

I can pray a breath prayer, *Let me see with Your eyes,* when—

- I feel that my children are headed in the wrong direction.

- they do something foolish.

- friends have a negative influence over them.

- they insist on having things their way.

- I know they are not being responsible.

- I am perplexed by a personal problem.

    Let me see with Your eyes.

QUIET MY HEART BEFORE YOU, FATHER.

The quiet words of a wise person are better than the shouts of a foolish king.

ECCLESIASTES 9:17 NLT

A quick review of today's schedule and you're already tuckered out. It's not enough that you already have half a dozen errands to run, housework to do, and dinner to prepare. Your child reminds you of the soccer game right after school and needs help with a science project—which is due tomorrow. No wonder you sometimes feel that you don't know if you're coming or going.

Perhaps you're tempted to scream, "Lord, where is that husband You gave me?"

Stop for a moment, and take a deep breath. Talk to God about your need to have your husband help out more.

96

Then listen for a moment. God heard your prayer, and you can trust Him to make things run smoother in your already-busy life. That includes His ability to help your husband see ways that he can help. In the meantime, let God help you do the next item with His guidance.

The role you play as a mother is an important one. With His help, you can do everything that is placed before you.

I can pray a breath prayer, *Quiet my heart before You, Father,* when—

- I don't know what to do next.

- the walls seem to be closing in on me.

- there are too many decisions to make.

- I have more on me than I can handle.

- everything seems to be a top priority.

- I am tempted to become frustrated with those around me.

Quiet my heart before You, Father.

MAKE ME A PEACEMAKER.

*Blessed are the peacemakers: for they shall
be called the children of God.*

MATTHEW 5:9 KJV

Don't you get tired of all the hatred in the
world? Everywhere you look, you can see
evidence of it—nation warring against nation,
ethnic cleansing, gang violence, lawsuits. Or
closer to home—sibling rivalry, family strife,
divorce. People have a hard time getting along
with others. One act of hatred seems to breed
more and more.

You wonder how you can make a difference
when you are only one person and you have no
control over the choices others make. It's not
your responsibility to reconcile the whole world,
but from your little corner of it, you can pray
for peace. Learn healthy ways to resolve conflict,

and work at making peace with those who are at odds with you. Extend your hand to your enemy. Turn the other cheek. Help others reconcile their differences. Point people to God.

God performed the ultimate peacemaking act when He reconciled the world to himself. You can be a peacemaker, too, because He lives in you.

I can pray a breath prayer, *Make me a peacemaker*, when—

- there is strife in my family.

- there seems to be an impasse at work.

- a broken relationship needs to be mended.

- there is conflict that involves my children.

- others hurt me.

- I am tempted to gossip.

Make me a peacemaker.

LORD, I AM CONFIDENT IN YOU.

Do not tremble; do not be afraid.

ISAIAH 44:8 NLT

God's Word plainly tells us not to be afraid. Fear weakens and destroys our trust in His promise of provision and protection for us.

It is impossible to shield your children from all the danger and hurt that is in the world. To get them ready, you let them know that you will not always be at their side. Before you release them, you teach them how to avoid danger when they can and how to handle it when they have no choice.

Help them understand that the Lord is on their side (Psalm 118:6 AMP). No one and nothing has more power against them than their Heavenly Father's power to protect them. Demonstrate your confidence in God, and through your witness they will develop their own trust in God and learn not to be afraid.

I can pray a breath prayer, *Lord, I am confident in You,* when—

- my children are threatened.

- they are away from home.

- they are in a storm.

- they face the unfamiliar.

- they go to the doctor or dentist.

- I hear bad news.

- I know others are afraid.

Lord, I am confident in You.

LORD, HOLD MY HAND.

I the Lord your God hold your right hand;
I am the Lord, Who says to you,
Fear not; I will help you!

ISAIAH 41:13 AMP

Do you remember how when you were little, your parents held your hand when you crossed the street? Maybe your father's hand covered yours as you learned to grip a baseball bat, or your mother guided your hand as she taught you to stir cake batter or to wash dishes.

Your child puts their hand into yours because they trust you. They look to you to help, guide, protect, and provide for them physically, emotionally, financially, and spiritually. If their hand begins to slip from yours, your immediate response is to grasp it tighter.

As your children grow, you gradually loosen your grip and gently place their hands in God's hand. You let them know that Almighty God loves them and that they can trust God just as they have trusted you. God will not let anything snatch them from His hand (John 10:28).

I can pray a breath prayer, *Lord, hold my hand,* when—

- my children start to stray away from You.

- they are in danger.

- I face temptation.

- I have to let them go.

- others try to persuade me or my children to do something wrong.

- they are searching for answers.

Lord, hold my hand.

YOU ARE MY STRONGHOLD, FATHER.

*Be strong in the Lord and in
the strength of His might.*

EPHESIANS 6:10 NASB

Motherhood has a way of using up all you
have and leaving you feeling tapped out and
unable to face one more crisis. But God is your
Father and your protector; and even when you
are weak, you can hide yourself in His strength.

When the plumber charges too much and
your neighbor steps over boundaries, when your
friend takes unfair advantage of you and life's
events just bowl you over, you can rest in God's
strength. In fact, He would like you to do that
even when you feel strong and able to cope. So
pray this breath prayer to learn how to lean on

God's power and make it through all that your day throws at you. With God as your stronghold, you can grow in confidence and find yourself facing down greater and greater challenges.

I can pray a breath prayer, *You are my stronghold, Father,* when—

- I know I need to confront someone.

- my children have an off day.

- someone damages my property through carelessness.

- I wake feeling tired on a busy day.

- things at work are tense.

- my family depends on me.

You are my stronghold, Father.

LORD, I GIVE THANKS TO YOU.

*Enter into His gates with thanksgiving
and a thank offering. . . .
Be thankful and say so to Him.*

PSALM 100:4 AMP

The Israelites were in bondage to the
Egyptians for more than 400 years. Then, God
miraculously delivered them and promised to
take them to a new, rich land.

They rejoiced for a little while, but soon
they seemed to forget God's goodness and began
to grumble and complain. Instead of taking a
few days to reach their destination, their journey
took forty years. In fact, many of them died in
the wilderness, without ever having seen the
Promised Land.

The Bible warns us not to follow their
example (1 Corinthians 10:10). No matter what,

God's desire is for us to be thankful (1 Thessalonians 5:18).

When you are hurt or disappointed, think of something to thank God for. Remember that even though life is not good all the time, your Heavenly Father is always good (Psalm 34:8).

I can pray a breath prayer, *Lord, I give thanks to You,* when—

- plans I've looked forward to change.

- I am unable to have something I really wanted.

- my family disappoints me.

- I feel rejected.

- someone has hurt my feelings.

- someone else gets what I have been asking for.

- God keeps me from hurt, danger, and trouble.

Lord, I give thanks to You.

LORD, YOU ARE THE GOD OF ALL COMFORT.

"As a mother comforts her child,
so will I comfort you."

ISAIAH 66:13 NIV

Do you remember how soothing your mother's voice was or how reassuring your father sounded when you were a child and needed to know that everything was going to be all right? It did not matter how bad things were; if they said not to worry, that was good enough for you.

You have also experienced God's soothing voice and touch during stressful times. Because of that, now you can comfort and reassure your own child when he is uneasy.

When your child is troubled, assure him that

God is well aware of it—that He is right there whenever a kind word or loving touch is needed. Rest at ease, knowing that God's rod and staff will protect, guide, and comfort your child (Psalm 23:4 AMP) just as He has done these things for you.

I can pray a breath prayer, *Lord, You are the God of all comfort,* when—

- my feelings are hurt.

- my children are troubled.

- I do not understand why bad things happen.

- friends do not seem to care.

- I need someone to talk to.

- I hurt because my child is hurting.

- I am afraid.

Lord, You are the God of all comfort.

GOD OF WISDOM, OPEN MY HEART TO YOUR INSIGHT.

The Lord will give you understanding in everything.

2 TIMOTHY 2:7 NASB

When your baby says their first words, you are so happy that you can hardly wait to tell family and friends. As their vocabulary increases, you begin to understand each other better. When they learn something new, they are eager to tell you in their own words and you both celebrate their accomplishment.

Just as you pray to understand God's Word (Psalm 119:73 NIV), ask Him to help you understand your child so that you keep the lines of communication open. Let your child know you want to understand them. When miscommunication occurs or there is a misunderstanding, you can go to God together and ask Him to help you understand each other.

I can pray a breath prayer, *God of Wisdom, open my heart to Your insight,* when—

- we do not agree.

- I am angry.

- others do not understand.

- my children try to explain their actions.

- they can't remember what happened.

- they feel I don't understand them.

God of Wisdom, open my heart to Your insight.

FILL ME WITH YOUR JOY, FATHER.

*Gladness and joy will overtake them,
and sorrow and sighing will flee away.*

ISAIAH 35:10 NIV

The unending demands of motherhood can leave with no energy left to feel happy. You know you've felt better at other times, but lately all the days feel gray and overwhelming.

God doesn't want you to suffer this way and He is there—always there—to help. In fact, His presence is where the joy of life comes from. The fruit of His Holy Spirit living inside you is joy according to Galatians 5:23. Many Christians have testified of moments when they felt God draw near, bringing light and joy into their lives. Go to Him and lay the gray day in His hands.

Let Him fill your life with color and vibrant
energy.

I can pray a breath prayer, *Fill me with Your joy,
Father,* when—

- I feel sad.

- my life feels dark and joyless.

- meeting my children's needs has used up
  all my energy.

- I realize I've forgotten what fun is.

- it has been cloudy all week long.

- a dear friend moves away.

  Fill me with Your joy, Father.

I DELIGHT MYSELF
IN YOU, LORD.

Delight yourself also in the Lord,
and He will give you the desires and secret
petitions of your heart.

PSALM 37:4 AMP

Have you ever had a day in which your
child seemed to enjoy being with you, doing
whatever you were doing? Remember how you
felt so close to them, and it was so easy to say
yes to their every request because they were in
harmony with you, and you with them?

In the same way, God feels joy when you
spend time with Him, paying attention to what
He is doing, helping out when you see something
you can do in His Kingdom. And sometimes in
the midst of your making Him the center of your
heart, your dreams come true. The Bible tells us
life with God can be like this.

Pray this breath prayer and think about how

good God is, how He has been kind to you in the past, how He is kind right now. Thank Him and enjoy being with such a kind and generous Father. You will find that He will give you dreams and make them happen.

I can pray a breath prayer, *I delight myself in You, Lord,* when—

- my day begins.

- my children snuggle close and remind me of Your love.

- I see the small wonders of nature outside my window.

- I have to move to a new location.

- things go wrong and I pull away to remember You are with me.

- there is cause for celebration.

I delight myself in You, Lord.

LORD, I TRUST YOU WITH THE FUTURE.

"I know the plans I have for you,"
declares the Lord, "plans to prosper
you and not to harm you,
plans to give you hope and a future."

JEREMIAH 29:11 NIV

You love your children very much and want only the best for them. Before they were born, you had already envisioned some of the good things you were going to do for them. Maybe you made definite plans or took certain steps to ensure a good life for them.

In His infinite love and wisdom, your Heavenly Father did the same thing for all of us. He mapped out His plans for you and your children before He created the world (Ephesians

1:4-5). God's plans for you and His plans for your children are "good and acceptable and perfect" (Romans 12:2 NASB). When you pray about your own dreams and encourage your children with theirs, think often about God's desire to bless you with His best.

I can pray a breath prayer, *Lord, I trust You with the future,* when—

- I wonder if my own dreams will ever come true.

- our financial stability is challenged.

- our children are discouraged about low grades in school.

- they are deciding on a career.

- others think they are a failure.

    Lord, I trust You with the future.

FATHER, IN YOUR WILL IS MY WORK.

Understand what the will of the Lord is.

EPHESIANS 5:17 NASB

Your zeal and good intentions have caused you to overfill your schedule with committee meetings and projects. Your child's school needs you to help out, and so does your church and your community—not to mention charities that solicit your help. You are glad to help, but how are you going to take care of your family and meet these other obligations too?

It would be easy to make excuses, cut a few corners, maybe miss a few meetings, or do a little here and there, just to get by. But you know God desires for you to work hard and cheerfully at whatever you do, as though you were doing it for Him (Colossians 3:23 NLT).

Since He knows what is best, ask what His will is. Say no when you should. And depend on God to help you do your best in the few things He lays out for you to do.

I can pray a breath prayer, *Father, in Your will is my work,* when—

- I obey You.

- I take care of myself.

- I take care of my family and our home.

- I do not have everything that I need or desire.

- I am not in a good mood.

- others do just enough to get by.

Father, in Your will is my work.

HOLY SPIRIT, YOU ARE MY GUIDE.

The Lord will continually guide you.

ISAIAH 58:11 NASB

Sometimes when people vacation in an unfamiliar place, they hire a guide. The guide will usually take them to the places that interest them most—places they will enjoy and that are safe. He wants them to have the best trip possible.

In a way, your Heavenly Father does the same for you by placing His own Spirit within your heart to guide you. He desires for you and your children to have the best life possible. He loves you and has your welfare at heart. When you learn to listen to His still small voice, you will be able to walk in His ways and train your children to walk in the destiny He has laid out for them. You will have His active help when things get confusing or children go through difficult times, especially during their teenage years. Let God's Holy Spirit be your Guide.

I can pray a breath prayer, *Holy Spirit, You are my Guide,* when—

- confusion and chaos make it hard to know what is right.

- I am forced to make difficult choices.

- my children are tempted to step off Your path.

- my children hide the truth from me.

- I feel alone and need to made a big decision.

- my friend asks for help with a complicated situation.

    Holy Spirit, You are my Guide.

LORD, YOU ARE
MY PROVIDER.

*My God will supply all your needs according to
His riches in glory in Christ Jesus.*

PHILIPPIANS 4:19 NASB

As you watch your husband quickly gulp his
morning coffee, you have second thoughts about
asking how things are going at his office. You
decide that his company's possible downsizing
has been the topic of conversation in your home
too much lately. Instead, you smile, give him
kiss, a hug, and whisper a prayer as he rushes
out the door.

You hear your newborn cry and you head
to the nursery. When you pick them up, they
immediately stop crying, satisfied with the attention that you provide.

Suddenly, you are aware of God's presence.
He reminds you that He is your Provider and

that He will take care of your family's every need. His power to provide is greater than any threats of downsizing.

God desires for you to go to Him and not depend on someone else when you are in need (Jeremiah 17:5). He is well able to take care of your family.

I can pray a breath prayer, *Lord, You are my Provider*, when—

- others offer to help.

- I am tempted to depend on others.

- money is running low.

- my husband and I plan our financial future.

- our income is less than our outgo.

- I want something I can't afford.

Lord, You are my Provider.

LORD, BE MY HELP.

*Since I am afflicted and needy, let the
Lord be mindful of me. You are my help and
my deliverer; Do not delay, O my God.*

PSALM 40:17 NASB

If you are a full-time homemaker, God does
not want you so consumed with caring for your
family that you wear yourself out. And if you
also work outside the home in addition to home-
making, your responsibility to keep yourself
healthy and able to serve is doubly important. It
is unhealthy for you and your family if you carry
more than you were meant to. Ask your
Heavenly Father to help you. Jesus invites you to
go to Him when you are weary and heavy-laden.
He promises that He will lift your burden and
give you one that is light and easy.

So when things get too hard and you feel

overwhelmed, go to the One who can arrange to lighten your load and strengthen you to carry what must be carried.

I can pray a breath prayer, *Lord, be my help,* when—

- I am tired from working at home or on a job.

- my children need attention and discipline.

- we entertain guests.

- I am sick.

- I am emotionally spent.

- I have taken on more than I can handle.

Lord, be my help.

LORD, I PLACE MY TRUST IN YOU.

God . . . freed me from my anxious fears.

PSALM 34:4 MSG

Frequent news about disasters, terrorism, and kidnappings has begun to trouble you. You feel fear creeping over you when you drop your child off at school. Unfamiliar noises make you jumpy. And when your husband is out of town, you might check your doors or the security system two or three times before you go to bed. You realize that if you do not get a grip on yourself, you will be afraid to walk out your front door.

You begin to pray and read the Bible more because you realize that you need the assurance of God's presence. Your Heavenly Father has

told you not to be afraid—not to even tremble—
because He is your God and He is with you
(Isaiah 41:10 CEV). Trust Him to protect and
keep your family safe. Remember His faithful-
ness, and it will help you stay free from fear's
clutches.

I can pray a breath prayer, *Lord, I place my
trust in You*, when—

- I am at home alone.

- I am driving down a long dark road.

- I hear about a bad accident and my
  family is not at home.

- I hear strange noises at night.

- I hear bad news reports.

- the doctor says that I need medical
  treatment right away.

Lord, I place my trust in You.

YOU ARE
FATHER OF US ALL,
LORD MOST HIGH.

*"I will be a father to you, and you shall be sons
and daughters to Me," says the Lord Almighty.*

2 CORINTHIANS 6:18 NASB

You know the wonderful, warm feeling you
experience when one of your children turns and
helps their sibling in a very tender way?
Suddenly it feels like sunshine came out from
behind clouds and that this is what you thought
being a family was all about.

God feels that way, too, only His family,
which includes you, is very large. As you go
through your day, look at your family, your
neighbors, the people on the street, and pray this
breath prayer. You will find yourself feeling con-

nected and wanting to treat those around you with great tenderness. And you will experience God's joy in His people and His creation when you give in to that desire.

I can pray a breath prayer, *You are Father of us all, Lord Most High,* when—

- I become aware of pressures in my husband's life.

- I see my neighbor out in her yard.

- I am in a group and feel lonely.

- I see someone begging in the street.

- I am caught in a traffic jam with lots of impatient drivers.

You are Father of us all, Lord Most High.

I WANT TO
ABIDE IN YOU, JESUS.

*"I am the vine, you are the branches; he who
abides in Me, and I in him, he bears much fruit,
for apart from Me you can do nothing."*

JOHN 15:5 NASB

If you read women's magazines or watch
talk shows, you can begin to feel small and
insignificant. You are not like the amazing mother of ten in one article or the mother of toddlers
who just succeeded in establishing a multimil-
lion-dollar business in another.

But God has plans for you that may not
make a magazine cover, but are very important
to the kingdom of heaven. Feeling daunted? You
shouldn't. God himself plans to create within
you the kind of strength and character needed to
fulfill those plans. All you need to do is learn to
abide in Him. Rely on Him to do what you cannot do. Live in such a way that you spend your

days talking to Him, listening to Him, and just plain leaning on Him. He will show you how abiding in Him will turn you into a channel of His strength.

I can pray a breath prayer, *I want to abide in You, Jesus,* when—

- I long to be more than I am right now.

- my children have used up my time and energy.

- my abilities seem to be hidden from others.

- I struggle with jealousy when others succeed.

- I recognize Your love for me.

- things do not go as planned.

- I must make an important decision.

  I want to abide in You, Jesus.

LORD, LET ME SEE YOU THROUGH THE EYES OF A CHILD.

Whoever will humble himself
therefore and become like this little child
[trusting, lowly, loving, forgiving]
is greatest in the kingdom of heaven.

MATTHEW 18:4 AMP

God calls you His child, so what type of father does He look like through your eyes? Imagine that you are a child and you are telling your friend how great your Father is. Maybe you would say:

"He loves me and He always tells me so. He takes good care of me and gives me good things. He likes talking to me. He teaches me what is right because He doesn't want me to get hurt or get into trouble. If I do get into trouble, He is right there to help me.

"He is always with me and He doesn't want me to be afraid. He wants me to be happy. He forgives me when I mess up, and He doesn't keep talking about it. I trust Him because He tells the truth and He always keeps His word."

Only you know how dear your Heavenly Father is to you. And if it is hard for you to find just the right words to describe Him, maybe the best way is to say it in the words of a child: "I've got the best Daddy in the whole world!" (Ephesians 4:6 NLT). And you would be telling the truth.

I can pray a breath prayer, *Lord, let me see You through the eyes of a child,* when—

- I take life too seriously.
- I lose hope.
- I do not know what to do.
- I need a friend.
- I need someone to hold my hand.
- I need someone whom I can trust.

Lord, let me see You through the eyes of a child.

HELP ME TO STAND BOLDLY, LORD.

The righteous are bold as a lion.

PROVERBS 28:1 NASB

Bullying. Abuse. Harassment.

Your child deals with these things at school. Your husband may face them on the job. Even you have dealt with them in some form— whether it was in the line at the local grocery store or while eating at a restaurant. Or, you might know of others whose lives have been strongly affected by such terrible treatment.

It is hard to understand how some people can be so cruel. But it's comforting to know that God has nothing to do with such actions because He is a God of love.

Even as a youngster, David knew what his rights were as a believer in God. That is what enabled him to stand boldly before the giant,

Goliath, and eventually slay him.

Study the Bible to know your rights as a child of God, and then stand on those rights. But make sure your attitude and your behavior are in order. Trust God to take care of you and to help you stand boldly in each situation in order to have God's very best for your life.

I can pray a breath prayer, *Help me to stand boldly, Lord,* when—

- I am mistreated.
- I am asked my opinion.
- someone tries to push me around.
- I have to speak in public.
- I must speak out against wrong.
- I feel that I am right.
- I have questions.
- I am placed in charge.
- I ask for a pay raise.

Help me to stand boldly, Lord.

LORD, MAY I WALK IN THE POWER, LOVE, AND DISCIPLINE OF YOUR SPIRIT.

[He has given us a spirit] of power and of love and of calm and well-balanced mind and discipline and self-control.

2 TIMOTHY 1:7 AMP

You are headed home after a tough day at work and feel a tension headache coming on. To your surprise, your husband has invited his supervisor to dinner this evening, and you have a project report due tomorrow. But this is only the beginning of your problems.

Next, you get caught in stalled traffic on your way to the grocery store. And when you finally get home, you see your dog's muddy paw prints all over the carpet and furniture. As you're cooking, your supervisor calls with questions about the project. While you're answering his questions, the lamb chops burn. Your guest will arrive in 30 minutes!

You cannot take anymore! You feel like screaming and pulling out your hair! Thank God that you have the presence of mind to go to your bedroom and pray. Only He can help you keep your emotions in control and get you out of this crisis (Psalm 91:15). You take a deep quiet breath and whisper, "Thank You, Lord."

I can pray a breath prayer, *Lord, may I walk in the power, love, and discipline of Your Spirit,* when—

- the unexpected happens.
- I have too much on my plate.
- plans do not turn out the way I think they should have.
- I made a commitment and did not write it down.
- my new hair color looks awful.
- I approach a driver's license checkpoint and realize my license is in my other purse.
- I burn my meal and my guests will arrive shortly.

Lord, may I walk in the power, love, and discipline of Your Spirit.

BE MY FRIEND, JESUS.

"I no longer call you servants, because a servant does not know his master's business. Instead, I have called you friends, for everything that I have learned from my Father I have made known to you."

JOHN 15:15 NIV

It's easy to feel isolated and alone when you are at home with small children. And when your children go off to school and become fascinated with their own friends, you can feel like a waitress, housekeeper, and chauffeur who is used but not appreciated.

This is why it is good to spend time every day with the One who loves you for yourself and who delights in the way He made you. When you feel small and insignificant, remember that the God of the universe has chosen to be your friend and to call you His friend.

On lonely days, pull your knees up on the couch. Put a cup of coffee by your side and spend time reading your Bible, God's love letter to you. And tell God the things on your heart. He really is your Friend.

I can pray a breath prayer, *Be my Friend, Jesus,* when—

- no one notices me.

- I've spent several days alone with my children.

- my husband has been too busy to talk with me.

- I'm kept from my own friends because the children are sick.

- I feel unlovable today.

- I am lonely.

Be my Friend, Jesus.

LIFT MY HEART WITH LAUGHTER, LORD.

A happy heart is good medicine and a cheerful mind works healing.

PROVERBS 17:22 AMP

Have you ever noticed how a good laugh can change your whole disposition?

You may have just come through one of the most horrendous days ever. The kids wouldn't behave. The washing machine broke in the middle of a wash cycle and you had to drain it by hand. Your husband called and has to work late—again!

In the midst of all this frustration, you flip on the TV and see a commercial that causes you to laugh uncontrollably—so much so that in a few moments you've forgotten about your troubles. You feel a renewed strength.

The famous writer Mark Twain once said:

"The human race has one really effective weapon, and that is laughter." In truth, God has given you many powerful weapons (2 Corinthians 10:4). But laughter is certainly one of them.

When you have one of those days when nothing seems to go right, ask Him to help you remember something that will make you laugh.

And then laugh. It will give your heart a lift.

I can pray a breath prayer, *Lift my heart with laughter, Lord,* when—

- I am disappointed.

- plans change and something I looked forward to is cancelled.

- something of value is accidentally broken.

- my family is sick.

- others around me are depressed.

- I make a mistake.

- my family doesn't offer any support.

Lift my heart with laughter, Lord.

FATHER, HEAR MY PRAYERS FOR MY CHILD.

Lift up your hands to him in prayer.
Plead for your children.

LAMENTATIONS 2:19 NLT

There is perhaps no greater joy than to be a mother. From the moment you discovered you were going to have a baby, your heart's desire and purpose was for your child's good health and happiness—throughout life. You are determined to spare no expense for their success. You feel confident that you are doing your best in planning and preparing for their welfare.

You want God's best for them, and prayer makes that possible. It goes beyond the natural boundaries and reaches the heart of God. Ask your Heavenly Father to help you be sensitive to

His promptings to pray for your child and to reveal anything specific that you need to pray about. Trust Him to help you pray as much and as often as you should, and thank Him for answering your prayers.

I can pray a breath prayer, *Father, hear my prayers for my child,* when—

- they are still in my womb.

- they are asleep.

- they are in school.

- they are challenged in their witness for You.

- they begin to drive.

- they have struggles that they haven't told me about.

Father, hear my prayers for my child.

SHOW ME SOMETHING NEW, LORD.

*"Behold, I will do something new,
now it will spring forth;
will you not be aware of it?"*

ISAIAH 43:19 NASB

God is a creative Being who can help you in
ways you wouldn't even know to ask for. Are
you having a problem that has kept you baffled
for years? Go to God and ask for something new
that only He can come up with for a solution.
He will surprise you with the simplicity of His
solution. Sometimes His answer may challenge
you to make adjustments you hadn't ever
dreamed of making. But trust the creativity of
His ideas.

Maybe you love to create and you'd love to
have God work with you on a project. Go

ahead. Ask Him for something new—a new approach, a new arrangement. He will be delighted you asked.

I can pray a breath prayer, *Show me something new, Lord,* when—

- I feel bored with the things around me.

- I'm facing a stubborn problem.

- I'm having trouble understanding a friend.

- I'm feeling the desire to create something.

- I want to see the world through Your eyes.

- I need help on a project for work.

   Show me something new, Lord.

MY EXPECTATION IS FROM YOU, GOD.

*My soul, wait silently for God alone,
for my expectation is from Him.*

PSALM 62:5 NKJV

You just finished studying really hard for a mid-semester exam and are expecting to make a high score. Or your supervisor is very pleased with your job performance, so you are expecting a raise. Maybe, after years of praying, you just found out that you are expecting your first child.

There is something exciting about expectancy. You believe that something good is about to happen and you wait in anticipation. It is easy to expect good things to happen when you know that you have done what is right to cause it to be so. But what about when you make a mistake, or suppose you have problems?

Do not fret over it. Trust God's love and mercy. He is your hope. You can still expect to receive and enjoy His goodness to you. Just like Job, your end will be better than your beginning.

I can pray a breath prayer, *My expectation is from You, God,* when—

- I face financial difficulties.

- my job is threatened because of a downsizing.

- my children are still very young.

- the economy is looming out of control.

- nothing seems to be going right for me.

- my future looks bleak.

- others are worried about the future.

My expectation is from You, God.

LORD, HELP ME LOOK FORWARD.

[Forget] the past and [look] forward to what lies ahead.

PHILIPPIANS 3:13 NLT

How often do you bring up incidents from your past? Probably a lot if you're talking about accomplishments such as being the most popular student in your class, leading the cheering squad, or scoring high on your college entrance exams.

But most likely you don't talk about things you did in the past that make you ashamed. And that's good.

God wants you to be focused on today. Expect His goodness today and every day and look forward to the plans and purposes He has for your life.

When, in disobedience to God's instruction, Lot's wife looked back at Sodom and Gomorrah after God's angel helped their family to flee that wicked place (Genesis 19), she was turned into a pillar of salt. You could say she never escaped her past.

Whether your past was good or bad, it is still your past. There is nothing about it that you can change, so don't stay there. Look to the present and the future. That's where God is. He has something better for you waiting there.

I can pray a breath prayer, *Lord, help me look forward,* when—

- I need to encourage myself.
- a longtime friend wants to bring up the past.
- I am disappointed with my present life.
- my future seems uncertain.
- I am tempted to remember my past mistakes.
- I return home to visit family and friends.
- I feel a loss for what used to be.

Lord, help me look forward.

I REST IN YOUR MERCY, FATHER.

Give thanks to the Lord, for he is good!
His faithful love endures forever.

1 CHRONICLES 16:34 NLT

Have you ever done something wrong, only to have someone say, "Oh, that's OK. We all make mistakes"? Maybe you bumped someone's car in the parking lot and they waved you on with a smile. Or perhaps you dropped the change you were putting into a customer's hand, it rolled onto the floor, and they just laughed about it.

It is a good feeling to know that there are people in the world who express love, kindness, and mercy—especially in times when you know you don't deserve it.

That type of response is much like what happened when Christ Jesus died for your sins.

You were forgiven. Your charges were cancelled and your debt was paid in full. God loves you and is always ready to show you mercy. His mercies are new every morning, because He knows that every day there is a possibility that you will fall short or do something that will require His mercy.

I can pray a breath prayer, *I rest in Your mercy, Father,* when—

- I make a mistake.

- I cause problems for others.

- I ignore Your voice and do something my way.

- I speak or act before I think.

- my mistakes cause problems for others.

- others refuse to show me mercy.

I rest in Your mercy, Father.

JESUS, MAKE ME A LOYAL FRIEND.

*A friend is always loyal, and a brother
is born to help in time of need.*

PROVERBS 17:17 NLT

You are so busy taking care of your family
that you sometimes wonder when you will have
time to have a life outside of your home. Your
family knows that you love them and that you
take good care of them, so they will not feel
threatened if you develop good friendships and
relationships. The key word is good.

You know that God loves you and that He
desires only good things for you. You enjoy the
relationship that you have with Him and you
want to extend that into Godly relationships
outside of your family and church.

Sometimes you cannot avoid dealing with difficult people. During those times when you do not have a choice in the matter—such as a job situation—pray for God's grace and help. Otherwise, prayerfully and wisely choose friendships and relationships that have a Godly influence and a positive impact on your life.

I can pray a breath prayer, *Jesus, make me a loyal friend*, toward—

- my husband and children.

- other family members.

- church members.

- neighbors.

- coworkers.

- business associates.

- others whom You want me to touch with Your love.

Jesus, make me a loyal friend.

SAVIOR, LIFT UP
MY HEAD.

God . . . you lift my head high.
PSALM 3:3 MSG

Oh, no! You made a slip of the tongue and your child heard you. You apologized to them and asked God's forgiveness, but now you are worried that they might not respect you and think that you are a phony.

A college friend who knew you when you were an alcoholic has just been hired to work in the same office as you. Will she mock you when you tell her that you are a Christian and you no longer drink? You are concerned that she will tell your coworkers and ruin your good reputation. Will your Christian testimony be destroyed?

Shame. Embarrassment. Regret. Guilt. They

all have a way of raising their heads and making you put your head down. But take heart because there is no condemnation for those who are in Christ Jesus (Romans 8:1). Your Heavenly Father lifts your head and crowns you with love and compassion (Psalm 103:4). He is not ashamed to call you His child. Lift up your head!

I can pray a breath prayer, *Savior, lift up my head,* when—

- I feel ashamed of my past.

- I feel guilty.

- I regret wrong decisions.

- I feel depressed or sad.

- others refuse to forgive me.

- others try to embarrass me.

Savior, lift up my head.

DRAW ME CLOSE TO YOU, LORD.

*Come close to God and
He will come close to you.*

JAMES 4:8 AMP

There is something comforting about being held close. You feel warm, secure and loved. Regardless of what is happening, it seems that the whole world is shut out and all the attention is on you. For the moment, you are all that matters.

Your child feels like that when you hold them and you feel the same when your husband holds you in his arms. Your Heavenly Father runs the universe, but He knows when a sparrow falls to the ground (Matthew 10:29). His eyes move to and fro throughout the earth, and He will certainly come and see about you

(2 Chronicles 16:9).

Do not wait until a problem or trouble arises to draw close to Him. Every day, reach up to Him and feel His wonderful presence surround you in love.

I can pray a breath prayer, *Draw me close to You, Lord*, when—

- my husband is out of town.

- my child grows up and does not need me as much.

- I am separated from my family.

- I feel lonely.

- others reject me.

- I cannot seem to feel Your presence.

Draw me close to You, Lord.

HELP ME TO KNOW HOW MUCH I MEAN TO YOU, FATHER.

May [you] know what is the hope
of His calling, what are the riches of the glory
of His inheritance in the saints.

EPHESIANS 1:18 NKJV

This may be the week you feel less than valuable, less than significant, and in fact you may feel less than lovable at the moment as well. But while you are at your worst, even then God sees you as a gift He has given himself at great cost, with no regrets about the cost. The Bible talks about God as the pearl of great price. But we rarely realize that to Him we are the pearl of great price that He sold everything He had to buy, and then He called it a bargain.

Motherhood carries some huge challenges,

and juggling motherhood with a job, other family relationships, and church responsibilities can leave you feeling as if you will never measure up. It is the most humbling profession in the world. So sink your roots into God's love for you—because that is how you will find the strength to keep on going.

I can pray a breath prayer, *Help me to know how much I mean to You, Father,* when—

- I've taken last place all week.

- I feel forgotten.

- I've been mistreated by others.

- my children don't respect me.

- I'm lonely.

- I'm restless, fearful, and dissatisfied.

Help me to know how much I mean to You, Father.

Additional copies of this book and
other titles by Honor Books
are available from your local bookstore.

Breath Prayers
Breath Prayers for African Americans
Breath Prayers for Women

If you have enjoyed this book,
or if it has impacted your life,
we would like to hear from you.

Please contact us at:

Honor Books,
An Imprint of Cook Communications Ministries
4050 Lee Vance View
Colorado Springs, CO 80918

www.cookministries.com